ONE HAND
IN MY
POCKET

And the Other One's
Holding a Sunflower

Written by Catherine Carroll

ONE HAND IN MY POCKET

By Catherine Carroll

Copyright © 2020 Catherine Carroll

ISBN: 9798567053744 (Paperback)

For more information about the author, Catherine Carroll, please drop her an email: csg4285@outlook.com

I dedicate this book to every single person that has reached out to me since my last book – the women going through the break up and the men having an insight into the woman's perspective. I also dedicate this book to everyone who is taking the journey to find their own inner heaven.

This is also an acknowledgement to the connection queen, Kate Robert's – her writing group for providing me with the space to connect into my soul and write from the heart, our giggly phone calls, and our shared dislike of orchids are what have made this year's lockdown memories.

My son, Lewis – what a funny, caring and best friend he has turned into. I am so glad I get to have him all to myself half the week. I absolutely adore him and am proud of him every single day.

My mum for having my little dog, Chico – she has made it possible for me to go to work and be happy that he is being looked after. This little dog has provided me so much love and that is only possible because he is happy.

'Your mind can be either your prison or your palace. What you make it is yours to decide.'

Bernard Kelvin Clive

Contents

Introduction

The title for *One Hand in my Pocket* came to me around three years ago. It was a passing thought of, *if I ever write a book, that's what I would name it*. If you are a fan of Alanis Morrissette you will know this is the title of one of her songs. For me, this song represents my life – I see my life as one big juxtaposition, a comparison between two dissimilar things by placing them side by side.

My life, at times full of many wonderful people, then empty and lonely. Belly laughs and a heart full of love with a shadow of shame and sadness. Full of energy, feeling alive, and then days spent lying in bed unable to move. But what it all comes down to is that everything is going to be alright.

I have had many people approach me for the magic formula to having a balanced life, how to be resilient, or how to get through heartbreak. I don't have all the answers, just a formula that works for me. I have studied, listened, watched, read, attended many *many* varieties of self-help resources. My journey initially began back in 2003 when I was in the final year at university studying for my psychology degree. A friend handed me a book, *Conversations with God* by Neale Donald Walsch. There was no reason she gave me this book. She said I would like it, and I did. From there I've continued my journey of self-development. It becomes quiet addictive and exciting to see "what's next".

My biggest transformations have come from times when I have listened, *truly* listened, to my inner voice, my inner child, the universe and, of course, my own judgements.

How do I manage to listen? I meditate and then meditate some more.

This does not mean sitting around on a mat humming OMMMMM (although sometimes it does). I can meditate whilst cooking, whilst walking my dog, whilst taking a shower, or listening to music. It's about tuning in and listening, being present, listening to the gaps between the sounds. The silence is often where my answers live.

Then there is radical self-love. I can get lost in the magic of the human body and its ability to repair, to function, to create, to cause us pain, to provide us comfort. This task is something that takes practise and requires us to deal with our own mind's shadow side. Carl Jung, who founded the field of analytical psychology, would state that the human deals with the reality of the shadow in four ways: denial, projection, integration, and/or transmutation. Therefore, for me to deal with my

2

shadow side I look at which way I am dealing with my reality. Once I have that figured out then this tends to transmute into self-love. Obviously, this requires absolute honesty – not self-destructive talk but compassion.

Once I learnt to accept and love what I have and who I am, then life became easier. It's not about settling for my lot. It's about living in the moment and being present. This is a challenge and not easy. We can live life from the 'if only' place of regret, or the here and now and make the best of it. I can only be what I can only be. Others are not better than us, they are better at something. No one is happier than me but they are happier being happy. They are not more in love with them; they love how they feel when with them. Our hearts do not get broken but our own dreams or ideals do.

Our thoughts, imaginations, and fantasies can absolutely destroy us. Critical self-talk is a habit that becomes our normal, and if we don't keep it in check it will destroy every ounce of self-love. Our mind looks at memories for how to deal with the here and now, and if we have only have a bank of painful memories then that's what we go to. It's as though our mind is on a loop, repeating the same stories over and over, the same old chatter of *you are no good, you are stupid, you messed up again, no one loves you, people can't be trusted, everyone leaves etc.* I had a variety of things playing on my loop, 24-hour enemies sent from

3

the depths of hell. I needed to stop this barrage of self-hate before I turned to anti-depressants, alcohol, or cigarettes to silence them. I decided to invent a new loop or even mantra. I would tell myself "return to love" "return to love" over and over again. At first, I would be saying this phrase at every opportunity, shouting it out loud in the shower if I caught myself hating my body. An observer may call me crazy! I would catch myself with a negative thought and immediately say my phrase. I got so good at it I could say it halfway through a negative comment, stopping it dead in its track. Then the magic started to happen. I would be able to sense in my body when the negative comment was on its way and manage to say my phrase before it even landed. I reprogrammed my mind from one of disappointment and fear into one of kindness and love. I had created a nurturing and loving relationship with myself. I now use this trick when I get a "nasty" thought towards someone else. This made my divorce journey a whole lot easier and has not left me stuck on a merry-go-round of never-ending hatred (or in a typical rebound relationship that many of us don't realise we enter into).

I then wanted to take this whole adventure onto a new level and tune into what I call the old brain. This is the part of the brain that regulates basic survival functions, such as breathing, moving, resting, feeding, emotions, and memory. Our endless pursuit of pleasure ignores that the flow of life is painful – everything changes, people die, we experience pain as a result of being in the flow of life. The way in which we try and cope with these pains can cause more pain. I only need to sit back and look at the time I thought my house would provide happiness for me and make me feel worthy. I worked 60 hours a week to be able to buy what is, for now, my prison.

I became curious on how to bring genuine joy into my life. Not having an attachment to an outcome but to listen to my old brain. Not to have set exercise times but to dance, stretch, or move when my body needed it. To participate in breath work practises and release locked-in traumas from my body. To become more attuned to my magic, connecting to spirit guides that resonated with me. To go to the beach if my body craved it or walk in the forest.

I believe that we all have a journey to travel and that includes both pain and joy. I also believe we are the masters of how long we stay in each state. I hope my writings give you an insight into the possibility of living a life of joy and pain, wonder and boredom, love and hate, and embrace it because everything will always be fine.

'The less you open your heart to others, the more your heart suffers.'

Deepak Chopra

1.
Hot Chocolate

Love told me I am doing so well.
You see, we made a pact, me and love.
We promised to always return,
And we do.

It always feels so good.
Kinda like the hot chocolate in my heart.
I also worked out how to add toppings to my hot chocolate.
It's so easy to do, like the easiest thing ever.
All you do is give love away and it comes back as toppings –
Whipped cream,
Marshmallows,
Cherries,
The whole shebang.

Today I ended up with all sorts of toppings,
Even a cherry on top.
When I return home to my empty home,
No longer a family place,
Just a bed to sleep,
I take my time to enjoy my daily hot chocolate.

Sometimes I feel sinful –
I just want to sleep
Other times the sugary toppings make me wanna dance and do
TikTok shit.

This is my secret, this thing I do.
I don't know how I invented it but I am so glad I did.
I spend all day making my hot chocolate,
So if I show you love,
You now know you're the topping on my hot chocolate
And I thank you.

That lady today, the one with the sad face –
She gave me sprinkles,
Once I told her I was so happy that she sat next to me today.

My boss –
She gave me the whipped cream after I acknowledged how hard
she had worked.

My friend –
She gave me the cherries today as I sat and listened to her
worries about becoming a mum.
I watched her eyes fill with fear and tears but replaced with a
smile and thank you.

You may think I am crazy doing this each day,

And sometimes I just feel like a herbal tea instead,

But someone always provides the teabag,

Usually me with some kind words in the mirror.

2.
Who's in Charge

You are safe.
You can't trust life to be easy.
Easy is not what you are here for.
You are safe though.

Just remember you can always create the situation.
This may seem bizarre to those who don't know you.
You know you though,
And you know you can do whatever you want,
No limits.

Take yourself there in your mind,
Where ever you need to be.
The body doesn't know what the mind doesn't tell.

If your body feels scared
The mind's not telling it something –
It forgot to communicate.

Your body is telling the mind it's not safe,
When really the mind needs to tell the body

We're safe, all is good.
Always use the line of communication from mind to body,
Not the other way around.

Your body will say it's hungry when it's just had food.
Your body will say it's tired when it's done nothing but rest.
Your body will convince the mind it can't carry on when it's not
even begun.

What an amazing gift the mind is.
Use it well and it will take you places you thought were only
imaginable.

Once you fully crack this, the body will then begin to speak its
truth,
That gut feeling will become the compass.

3.
Thank You Step Mum.

Today he goes on his family holiday.

His new family that I don't even know.

It hurts me deep within that my boy has a life I don't belong to.

The worst part is that it's unnecessary, this secret family.

They see me as a woman scorned.

I am nothing that they believe,

I am grateful she is nice to my son.

Like really *really* grateful that I don't sit and worry that my son

has a wicked step mum.

I wish she would phone me and we could be friends.

She helped my husband leave me –

His wife,

His miserable life.

She has no idea she helped me too.

I thank her for making me sit up and find me.

The person I lost years ago.

She is back –

Here I am.

Thank you lovely step mum for caring for my son.

Because of you I now have free time that I used to feel guilty to even dream about.

I can now talk on the phone without him, the ex, listening in...

Oh wait, that's probably why we have never spoke.

I promise you one day –

I bet it's 'our' son's wedding day –

You will see me smile with gratitude in my eyes all for you.

4.
Work Lady

She has lost her shine.

Oh my gosh, what happened to this beautiful woman?

My work colleague from years back.

The one who never invited me to her wedding because?

I guess I wasn't trendy enough,

Not part of the shiny girl crowd or something at the time.

She was always so full of it,

So *bring it on* attitude.

So clued up,

The world in her hands.

The champion of us all.

But it's not there,

The light has gone out.

Just sadness and a sense of

I gave up,

I am tired,

This race is too long.

I listen to her tell me how work is a bag of shit.

She never used to talk about it like that.

I suggest maybe once lockdown is eased she will feel better
But nope, she doesn't think so.
Then we get to it ... another one lost into the vows of
"I take this man and lose every ounce of who I am."
"I take this man and let him mould me into a flat nothingness in his world."
"With this ring I thee forget who I am and run on the hamster wheel of, 'How can I help you, what would you like, am I pretty enough? Am I fun enough? Am I 'til death we do part or is it 'til I'm dead inside?'"

She is lost in the spare room at home,
I imagine her like an injured cat licking her paws
Trying to figure out what hurts.

I can see all the questions running around in her head,
All the self-blame and words of failure.
He was such a catch where did she go wrong?
She just shrugs her thin shoulders and says, "It is what it is."
Oh my, she is using my catch phrase.

I will look for her again at break time and I will wear my biggest heart and let her know how great she is doing because she is.
She has always done her best
But now she is doing her best to punish herself.

It's painful to see

But also necessary for this broken woman to realise

She's not you, Mr husband guy, she is me.

'Be the change you wish to see in the world.'

Mahatma Ghandi.

5.
Shoulda

The tears, they are here and then they go.
The laughter, it's here and then it stops.
The searching, it's here and it always stays.

Searching for the next level in this game,
The video game of life.
Should I stay in my job or move up a level?
Should I share my moments with someone?
Or am I just filling empty moments with empty shoulda stuff?

I don't have wants,
I have shoulds.
Should I do this?
Should I do that?
What should it be?

Shoulda been more happy.
Shoulda been more open.
Shoulda listened.
Shoulda seen the signs.
Shoulda been more feminine.

Shoulda been less masculine.

Shoulda been more empathic.

Shoulda been more caring.

Shoulda been a better friend.

Shoulda been more careful.

Shoulda taken it easy.

Shoulda done it different.

Shoulda seen it coming.

It should be whatever it needs to be, that's all.

Love tells me today –
It should only ever be that.

6.
Suicide Plan

He is there forever in my heart and mind.
With all the others that have gone before.
I know I am in his too,
The main character in the crossroads of life.

3 am he made the call,
Three days he had been walking the streets,
No sleep,
No food.
Three years since he walked out of his home,
Left his wife and children.
Without a reason,
Without a fallout,
Just his own tormented mind.

He was sat on a bench,
Photo of his children in his hand.
His words of sorries and goodbyes written on the back.
Like something out of an Eminem song.

I am not sure what he expected when he made the phone call to save him from his suicide plan.

Maybe the normal bullshit of a prescription of medication.

He got me though,

All of me in my full presence and integrity.

Wearing my uniform that screams out authority and
knowledge.

In reality, it's just a cloak to disguise my healing powers.

Just the two of us sharing an hour of life or death.

I loved him so much with every cell of my body and he could
sense that.

He knew he was safe,

No judgement from me.

Just me here in my power,

In full alignment of my purpose for that hour.

No script,

No policy was followed,

Me doing what's right not what suits the system.

Just words from somewhere else,

Somewhere beyond my mind.

We decided looking at the evidence that he was totally right and that *yes* he should end his life. Y

"Yes," I said, "let's do a suicide ceremony."

I could sense he didn't know if I was more crazy than he felt
But he was also in awe of my bravery.

Cause you have to be brave when suicide is involved.
No half arsed attempts,
It has to be full on commitment –
No turning back.
Without that you take the risk of being disabled,
Or relying on a machine to help you breathe.

He agreed to committing to his suicide and that it had to be fully
complete.
We had to end all the pain,
The fear,
The shame,
The lack of love.

So that's what we did,
We did a few deep breaths and put our hands on our hearts
And killed that old version of him ready for the new.

Not one ounce of blood loss,

Not one pill or rope around the neck.
We put his photo in his pocket and set about finding him a
hospital bed for the night.

We talked about how he was now going to face everything
And deal with it because he has already committed suicide
And you can't do it twice.
So those tougher days are just reminders of the life that died.

33 years old he was and starting again,
Being born into love rather than shame.

Not a drug or a drink in his system,
Just a lost soul looking for home.
A lost connection now a feeling of higher love.

I know he is safe and he always will be,
He will tell the tale of the night he committed suicide
And I can imagine him wondering if it was real
Or a dream and he just woke up in a hospital bed.

7.
Memory Box

Memories and smells, yes.
Memories and sounds, yes.
Memories and touch, yes.
Memories and sight, not so much.

How does it work this memory game?
Why do we take up so much room with them?
What are we without them?
An empty memory box?

My memory box is a jumble,
Not all neat and tidy.
Every memory mixed in with another.

A bit like a photo album with no dates or order.

Maybe this is why my memories aren't great when
remembering with sight,
It's hard to find them that way.

Selfies are good –

They don't have to be in order,
Just random snaps that capture the mood for me rather than the
occasion.

Maybe I am a mood collector rather than a memory box.
That's good, so long as I don't forget what love feels like.

8.
I Don't Love You

Love is not what you think it is.

It's a muddle of stuff.

A muddle of what people have told you love is.

He provides for me – he loves me.

She cooks for me – she loves me.

They invite me – they love me.

It's all clear, this love game.

It's me I love, not you.

I don't love you at all.

I love me when I am with you.

I love the smile on my face.

I love the floaty lightness of my body.

I love how I am when I am with you.

I now need to love how I am when I am with me.

I think I do … finally.

9.
I Don't Hate You

Hate is not what you think.

It's a muddle of stuff.

A muddle of what people have told you hate is.

He texted someone else – he hates me.

She didn't say goodnight – she hates me.

They didn't invite me — they hate me.

It's all so clear, this hate game.

It's me I hate, not you.

I hate me when I am not with you.

I hate the tears in my eyes.

I hate the heavy in my heart.

I hate how I am when I am not with me.

I hate how I am when I am not love.

'As grief pours out, love pours in.'

Rebecca Ann Wilson

10.
Bumpy Ride

I wish I could make you see.
It's not about them, it's about you.
Let them be, leave them alone.
They are travelling their own little road.

Don't say a word, do not judge.
Every judgement you make is bounced back to you from
someone else.
You know this –
Let them be.

Don't expect support and not give it back.
Don't expect the truth and then see it as an attack.
Sometimes your words make me cringe.
You use the excuse of honouring your feelings
But sometimes they lack integrity.
Who are you to sit in judgement,
In judgement of someone trying to figure it all out?

They don't claim to have all the answers
Just a journey travelled.

You don't have to participate.
You don't have to comment.
We are all experts on our journeys and they are in theirs.

This web of who has my back?
It's simple –
It doesn't matter, it really doesn't matter.

Appreciate what they do,
Even if its bullshit, let them be.
You don't have to join in or add to its energy.

Just smile and wave.
It's their road to travel,
So stop with the pot holes,
You're making it bumpy.

Shit, I just added some pot holes to your road...

I am sorry.

11.
Depression

We are going to spend one more day this way.

Just sitting about waiting for time to pass.

Snoozing like a lazy cat.

Having snuggles with the little dog.

It's a fine line between boredom and relaxing.

I feel shame to have wasted my time off work.

Not one book read.

Not one lunch with friends.

Not one ounce of make-up.

Just me, the dog, and snoozes.

From the outside it might be classed as depression

But it's not.

I am ok.

I don't want to see anyone or speak.

It's not because I am depressed,

It's just because I am with me.

I don't want their energies seeping into mine.

I don't want to have to smile and nod when they tell me their news.

I am not arsed about stock markets, pensions, vaccines,
Or whatever you like to talk about.

I am not some warrior on a mission to enlighten the world,
To make them love,
To make them see.

I would just rather lay here with my little dog and be free.

12.
No News

Love has nothing to say to me today.

No news, no revelations, nothing.

Maybe it will speak to me later…

When my boy comes home from his holiday.

When I see how much he has grown without me.

When I scan all his new freckles from the sun.

When I hear him squeal at all his favourite foods in the fridge.

When he finally says, "Goodnight mum, I love you,"

And we are under the same roof.

13.
Wise Old Woman

I have become a wise old woman.
I feel a little proud to take this badge.
Love gave it me yesterday.

The young mum to be,
Now a friend of yours.
Love is on its way to her,
Cooking in her belly.
She has to trust the process
And see it as just another natural process of her life.
I wish she would believe me when I tell her that her body will
take over and know exactly what to do.
Her mind will switch off –
No chatter,
No questions,
Just animal instincts

I can't explain to her this switch that happens.
It frustrates me that I sound like some witch talking about
magic.
But that's what it is magic.

This switch that we should have witnessed at some point in
childhood.
Then we would understand how powerful we really are.
Adulthood wouldn't be as worrying if we could see our sisters,
Our mothers,
Our friends
Take this journey from girl to mother.

Child birth –
The most natural thing ever
And we are hiding it away like a dirty secret.

Why is that, Love?
Why so hidden?
Why are women hiding away this power,
The crossing from one state to another?
A vulnerable time
Yet we just don't feel safe.

I wish I could teach this magical journey…
What are you talking about?
You did yesterday,
With Love!

14.
Plodder Lane

We are just plodding along at the moment.

Stuck in time.

No figuring stuff out.

No creating something new.

Just nothing –

Sleep,

Wake,

Sleep,

Wake.

Is this it? How it's going to be?

No highs.

No lows.

Being fully present to each and every moment.

No stories attached.

No attachment to outcomes.

Is today a glimpse of what being fully present to the moment is?

I'm not too keen,

It feels, well…

It feels like plodding.

I like the excitement of doing new stuff, I think.

I like the buzz of building a life of dreamy stuff, I think.

I love the initial getting to know someone, I think.

Maybe I'm not ready for Plodder Lane.

I think I will keep on thinking about stuff and just stay here on Fuck Knows Street.

15.
Magic Apples

I have this ability to see magic.

We all have it,

Some just don't use it.

I can look at someone or something and be in awe of

How amazing they are.

The apple seed planted in the ground.

Growing up into a big tree.

Producing its own offspring.

Magic apples free for you and me.

The magic apple sat in the fruit bowl on the kitchen side.

Just sat there,

Not sparkling,

Just being an apple,

Not expected to become a tree.

Why can't it see its magic?

Why doesn't it want to be a tree?

The lovely crunch I feel upon my teeth.

The sweet juice that gives me a sugary boost.

Thank you, little apple.
You mean so much to me.

16.
Worms

Did you feel me?
Did you notice me?
It was me,
It was Love,
Letting you know I am here.

I didn't think my love would feel like that.
I thought my love felt like that giggling laughter.
It felt like a worm in my chest.
Rising up,
A wriggly worm.

Oh, it all makes sense now!
That's how I survived on the worm meal plan!

"Nobody loves me, everybody hates me.
I think I'll go and eat worms.
Big, fat, skinny ones,
Tiny little shitty ones,
See how they wiggle and squirm.
You bite off their heads and suck out the juice

And throw their skins away.
Nobody knows how I survive on worms three times a day."

The worm diet –
It's really the Love diet.

FFS, I've been eating worms all my life!
No wonder they felt so tasty.

17.
Changes

The quiet of the house.
The noises that can be heard because it's quiet.
The loneliness off the rooms.
The sadness of the empty beds.
The lack of things being moved or touched.

The stillness of a broken home.
The pain of a broken world.
The sleepless nights that last forever –
They feel so sad but are so necessary.

But then it all ends and becomes –

The peace in my soul.
The content in my belly.
The warmth in my eyes.
The spreading about in the bed.
The doing what I want.
The only clothes pile being mine.
The singing of the birds.
The little dog wagging tail.

The fridge full of food only I like.

The never ending supply of books.

The clean bathroom.

The bank account I don't have to justify.

The relief at being single.

18.
Unlovable

He was so damaged,
She didn't stand a chance.

Happy family love was all he wanted,
But wouldn't allow.

Someone to love,
But she chose a man who didn't dare show.

Strong enough to see the love inside,
But just held in tight.

Forehead kisses in the night,
A window of love too afraid to show.

Wounds from childhood running deep.
People hurting all around,
Unable to see the damaged child.
Childhood pain being taken away
And then re-labelled as her pain for the day.

Fear and sadness hidden inside.

No point showing it to the blind.

19.
Peaceful Warrior

What is this magic?

It's keeping me awake.

The smell of his aftershave in my hair.

A reminder of the passion felt deep within.

The sensual kiss, so perfect, never to be forgotten.

How he held me gentle and strong in a way I had never known

before.

He felt so familiar but brand new too.

The Erikson handshake?

Soulmate connection?

Vision board manifesting?

My peaceful warrior?

Not for now,

I'm not ready for him yet.

'Our purpose is to be happy.'

Dalai Lama

20.
Grandma

It was beautiful,
It felt Italian themed.
Representing large family and togetherness.
Big tables all set perfect –
Big white plates,
Golden knives and forks.
Fresh white linen and large pink peonies.

Each table with name cards,
So many tables,
So many people.
All gathering together to celebrate your life.
I suppose with nine children and grandchildren in double
figures you touched a lot of people's lives.
I always felt like it was just you and me in the world though.
My grandma, the one who used to tell me I was more like a
daughter than a grandchild.

I couldn't find my name at the tables,
I didn't know where I belonged.
No one looking for me because I wasn't next to them.

Of course they aren't,

That's what *you* always did.

But now you are gone and it looks like I have gone with you.

I take a plate from the side and add a little bit of ham and bread.

I go and sit alone and eat my little picnic out of sight –

Alone but in your memory.

Then I wake up with tears on my pillow,

Missing you so much but grateful for the picnic reminder.

21.
WhatsApp Love

I sit here waiting,

Longing,

Hoping

For that sound.

That sweet sound *buzz buzz message received* from my sweet man.

It's an instant smile,

It's an instant jolt in my heart,

It's an instant 'my baby is here'.

It's so romantic, this twist in our journey,

Unable to touch,

Unable to speak,

Just heart felt words exchanged at random times.

It feels almost like praying

Then feeling the touch of God in your heart.

The touch of love,

Of oneness,

Of coming home.

It's a blessing in disguise,

Achance to appreciate what we don't have yet.
I never want to let you go –
Your home in my heart is there for good.
A golden thread connecting us heart to heart,
Weaved over the weeks through our words.
Getting stronger day by day.

My sweet man,
I await the *buzz buzz*.
Then I get bored and delete you.
What the hell is this online love?!

22.
Alone

Well, this a new –
Home from a date.
Lovely chat and getting to know each other.
Then the awkward home time.
Having to explain that I don't want to invite him in.
It's not a place for lust and one-night stands.
It's the place I always wanted loving hands.

Here I am,
All alone,
Crying,
No one to hold.
These tears,
Tears of alone.
Burning my face with loneliness.

The loneliness of a non-loving marriage
Now the loneliness of single life.

Is it worse than the loneliness of empty sex?
I don't think so.

23.
New School Year

We still need to decide what's next.

Oh yeah, Love, I forgot, sorry.

Ok, so what's next? What should we do next?

What should we do for the rest of the year?

Should we have fun, Love?

Hang on … what season is it?

Oh, you don't know either!

Hmmm…

I think more fun would make us tired.

Yeah, I agree. Hmmm.

What about being sad, should we be sad?

Christmas is coming up, it's always a good time to be sad.

Errr … no being sad!

Well, it just makes us sad.

It doesn't actually do anything worthwhile.

What about worry? Should we worry about everything and
worry if people like us and worry if we are healthy?

Definitely not!

We are not doing the frigging worry thing.

Holly shit –

That worry game is the pits.

We always lose!

Oh, I don't know Love, what should we do next?

What about a bit of study?

Oh yes, Love, my favourite way of being!

Let's learn all we can from now until Christmas.

Everyone we meet has to teach us one thing,

OK, not everyone we meet, that's too much learning!

Once a day, we have to learn a little something,

Either from a book, a person, an animal, or from ourselves.

Perfect, thanks Love.

School of NOW until Christmas is officially open.

24.
Loser

What's going on, Love?
Why do I feel this way?
I don't want to workout, things are hurting.
My knee, my neck, my legs, my arms, my body.
Do I need to change it up, take up swimming?

Oh, frigging hell, I hate swimming!
Always takes me back to that day.
The day of the gold swimming badge.
Swimming a mile after doing lots of duck dives in my pyjamas.

Swimming a mile, getting out of the pool with jelly legs.
Almost falling over whilst waiting for the
Golden badge of reward.
Looking at the instructor with her clipboard in hand.

"You failed on the first dive, go and get changed."

Not one bit of emotion from her, not one fuck given.
Not one bit of love or concern for the battle I had just done.
If she had made eye contact she would have seen my eyes,

Burning from the pool water and silent tears.

The first time in my life I realised no one cares if I win or lose,

Pass or fail.

25.

Surrender and Flow

He leads me with such laser focus and presence.
Never missing a beat, always gently guiding me back.
He knows where I should be, like a sixth sense he has.
He uses arm movements and nods of the head
To bring me where he wants me.
Like a dance between two people,
One relying on the other to lead.

Sometimes I just stare at him and my body moves as it needs –
It just gets it right.
Other times I look up and away,
Just so I can listen to his cues
And feel him guiding me with his voice.

Now and again we will mirror each other and we become
synchronised, in movement and in sounds.
Sometimes I become vulnerable and a little shy –
He sees it and reassures me.
He can read my body and mind like an open book.

Now and again we both get silly,

We laugh and laugh like best mates in the pub.

We are so perfect together, I can't explain it.
He makes me feels safe.

Then my time is up and I pay him for his time,
My drumming lesson is over
And I know he's no longer mine.

26.
Lost

What is the point of all this?

Am not talking life purpose stuff.

The daily grind, what's the point?

Get up, shower, go to work, pay bills, come home, go to bed.

It has no point apart from to keep a warm roof over my head.

A bed for my son albeit half the week.

Why am I wasting my life doing this stuff?

What should I be doing?

Where should I be?

Trading time for money.

Trading time for a tired body.

Am lost again.

Are we ever really free?

27.
Boundaries

They arrived late AGAIN.

It's always OK, though.

I am always early –

I can't cope with the stress of being late.

I can't let them down.

They will be worried something has happened,

They will be annoyed etc, etc.

Their lateness is always a double whammy for me because

Well, I'm always early.

I waited an hour yesterday,

My half hour early

And their half hour late.

I hadn't eaten because going to get food could have made me late.

They arrived –

No apology, just a barrage of moaning about the traffic

And how it's unfair.

The wounded late person.

And I just stand there saying it's OK.

Well, it's not OK is it?

I need to set boundaries for myself.

No more being early and putting myself through extra pain.

28.
The Prep

It's all temporary, don't worry, it will all pass.
Then the new will begin.
You should know this by now, Catherine.

The pain is for you to observe, it will pass.
But am I doing OK, Love?
Do I need to do anything?
Just observe and listen, that is all there is to do.

Oh, I hate this stage.
The observe and listen stage.
I am such a doer.
I also know this stage is the most important stage.

A bit like the prep stage when decorating.
Get this right, spend lots of time doing the prep, and the end
result is flawless.

Oh, I just realised why I am one of the messy people in life.

OK, Love, I will observe and listen.

29.
Nothingness

I have nothing to write today.

My words all dried up.

My pen full of invisible ink.

My creativity needing to meditate –

Meditation my creativity's version of red bull.

Today no writing.

Today is a day of reset

Last chance gone.

See you on the next page.

30.
Fresh Bedding

Thank you fresh bedding.
You make me feel so snug.

Thank you fresh bedding.
You feel so soft.

Thank you fresh bedding.
You smell so clean.

Thank you fresh bedding.
I had a lovely dream.

'Self care is how you take your power back.'

Lalah Delia

31.
Annual Leave

We didn't get it done.

All those things unfinished, some not even started.

Lunch dates with mates missed.

Phone calls and messages left unanswered.

Ironing pile growing.

Garden weeds overtaking.

Not one beach visited.

All my spare time now run out.

Time to shake things up.

A new job is what's calling.

A fresh set of faces.

A new bag of personalities.

Stepping up and out of my skillset into something unknown.

I'm going to own it like I always do till my enthusiasm runs dry.

Then I will walk away like I was never there.

32.
Clothes

Is it something I need to learn?

Wearing clothes –

What is this skill that women possess?

Putting colours and fabrics together with ease.

How do I manage it?

I love wearing my uniform,

Someone else's choice on what I look like.

I need to find a uniform for my days off.

My like of hand-me-downs and hate for shopping trips

Has left a big gap in my knowledge.

My clothes always someone else's choice.

What do I do about this, Love?

Does it matter?

I just can't figure it out.

I think someone once muttered, "Dress to impress."

Impress who?

The label chasing ones?

The nice reserved girl?

The other frumpy mums?

The yogic goddess?

The sporty instructor?

Why the need to impress?

Why not just feel comfy and protected?

I can't even find the comfy and protected look though.

33.
Jobs for the Boys

I know your game.

I am onto it guys.

I see your little Man Club with the badge jobs for the boys.

Thing is, I don't even want to be on your team.

You have nothing to fear.

I have been asked to help out, and that's all I am doing.

You're making it difficult, though.

Through your fears, your trying to make me fail.

I know you're giving me the toughest tasks.

I know I am wearing the heaviest equipment in the room.

I know you are using code language between each other.

Like I said, I know your game.

I don't have a game, though.

Frankly, I don't care about winning.

I am not competitive.

So crack on boys.

Keep yourself indispensable but also unpleasant.

Whilst I just grow a bigger dick

Than all of you dicks put together.

34.

Lemon Crunch Cake

I could sense you felt scared so I made small talk

About your lovely hair.

We instantly bonded,

I liked you straight away.

Then off you went for your procedure to be done.

Whilst you were on the table having the investigation

I waited for you.

The recovery bay –

My own little area of recovery that had turned into a little

therapy space too.

Before you joined me, the manager came and gave me sign of

bad news.

I nodded and then put my hands in prayer position,

And asked for protection of my heart whilst I held yours in love.

Out of theatre you came,

A little groggy from the sedation but OK.

I swear from that moment on I made sure that you felt like

The most important person

I had ever met.

I know the road you have ahead of you,
I know your world is switched upside down,
I know you will have so many regrets about covid keeping you
from your family when all along you were dying anyway.

How cruel,
What a horrible twist –
Months of isolation whilst the cancer grew
And now it's too late,
Nothing more can be done.

I made sure you left me with something happy to remind me of
you –
A recipe for your favourite cake.
The one you make for your son.

Then your son came for you
And you introduced me like a proud friend.
His face looked relieved that you were happy
And I wished you well.
I felt a twinge of sadness as you turned and waved
Whilst being led into the office for THE chat,
Still unaware that your world was near the end.

35.
Listen

Listen, listen, listen.

Stop and listen to your body.

It's screaming at you to listen.

It's crying its heart out.

Listen to your body, it's feeling beat.

It's talking all day long.

Listen to its wisdom.

Stop and listen.

Take time out, sit on a beach.

Swap the coffee for water.

Rest your weary feet.

Listen to your body.

Give it a chance to speak.

It's not asking for much in return.

Just the basics –

Warmth,

Comfort,

And something good to eat.

Listen to its whispers.

Disguised as spots and aches.

Listen to your body.

You have to work together.

Become the best performing act.

Give it the best part to play

As well as the most amazing seat.

36.
Reiki

You need to tighten your daily practise.

Today you did reiki at work –

Where do you think that message to tune in came from?

Now is the time to tune in each day.

That is all I have to say on the subject.

37.
Sneaking About

The other woman, that's what I feel like.

My son popping in before school.

A quick half hour of chatter and feeling relaxed.

I can see the weight lifting from his shoulders as soon as he comes through the door.

What's going on in his other home life, I wonder?

Is he being true to himself or is that not possible?

I guess that's his journey to figure out.

All I can do is hold and support.

In the meantime, I will be here in the place called home.

Then the phone calls start, from his dad.

He is on to him.

I can hear his voice in the background

And I am irritated by his presence in our stolen time.

I guess this is how she used to feel when I would chat on the phone to my then husband.

Strange how we all walk in each other's shoes for a while.

Off to school he goes with his mum fix for the day.

Until we see each other again, my boy.

I hope you learn to speak your truth today.

38.
Unsettled

Here we go again –
A barrage of messages all day long.
Asking me stupid questions.
Pretending to show an interest.

The narcissist is on the prowl again.
What is it he wants now?
What bomb shell is he going to drop?
Like a cat playing with a toy.
Bat bat
Gentle taps then
POW teeth sunk in.

He knows he is getting off lightly with this divorce.
I am not even asking to see his bank account,
The same account that's probably full of cash from our married years.
Cash he stored whilst giving me a small allowance from my salary.
I am not even asking him to pay any extra than his half on the mortgage.

I am not asking him to pay me any maintenance.

I am not even chasing his pension.

Stupid maybe but I don't want him to be part of my future.

I am not asking him anything…

But he continues to hound me today.

I feel sick,

I feel unsettled,

Not felt this for a while.

This feeling used to be so familiar

That I thought it was my norm.

Every day of being with him had me feeling this way.

Not knowing what I had done wrong,

Or if I had done right?

Only receiving attention if I was unhappy.

Nothing but looks of disapproval should I be happy.

The occasional snigger at me

But refusing to say what he found funny.

Like a reward system, Pavlov's dog.

Trained to be unhappy by its master.

But no longer a pet because

Now I run free.

I might even bite.

'Success is a function of alignment.'

Emily Johnsson

39.
Vanilla Ice Cream

Vanilla ice cream I love you.

Vanilla ice cream you are lovely.

Vanilla ice cream you are not plain.

Vanilla ice cream you cheer me up.

Vanilla ice cream I love you.

Vanilla ice cream your colour is like sun shine.

Vanilla ice cream you remind me I am loved.

Vanilla ice cream you are magic.

Vanilla ice cream you don't need a flake.

Vanilla ice cream thank you.

40.
Wounds

Good things have finally arrived.

I have a new trick.

No longer pretending to be brave.

I AM BRAVE.

I am in my power, full alignment.

What an amazing feeling it is.

No swampy reactions.

No justifications.

My boundaries clear.

No safe chatter.

My ego has left the building.

I have no fear.

Your ego doesn't hurt me or even cause worry.

I no longer feel small.

I no longer feel unworthy.

My voice is strong and can be heard.

I can tell you are puzzled and slightly annoyed.

Your childish chatter is giving it away.

Your power is now invisible.

My wound is healed.

My scar like your power –

I can't even see it.

41.
Divineness

We are brought together again,

Spending a couple of days working with each other.

Exchanging our time for money.

We just flow so well.

It's like a perfect partnership.

I provide him with everything he needs so he can perform.

We gather our energy and set the intention we want.

We add some giggles.

Little friendly jokes,

The patient becomes at ease.

I set up the equipment.

He waits for me to let him know I'm ready and we begin.

He lets me move round the room,

Be creative,

Chatter,

Hum,

And provide loving care to the patients.

All the time he remains still in and control,

Focused on his task.

He knows I won't distract him and I need to do my thing.

Come into my power whilst he holds the space.

He is quiet,

Very quiet.

I look at his face and see the concentration.

He has to get it right,

No second chances.

Then he relaxes and we are done.

I see the energy drain from him,

His muscle relax.

He becomes quiet and reflective.

It's a beautiful day each time we are together.

An insight into the perfect relationship

That's not co-dependent.

42.
Weirdos

Today is the day I leave home and arrive home.

A retreat full of weirdos.

A piece of me feeling like the biggest weirdo there.

Stepping out of my comfort zone yet again.

Dancing about, shaking my womb.

Feeling like an absolute dick head but also knowing it works.

Time to do more deep healing.

Time to shine light on the dark.

Time to be guided and held.

Time to be punched to my limits.

Time to switch on the magic.

Broken down and smashed into a billion pieces.

Then gently and precisely

Cleaning each piece

And putting it back together.

Thank you, Love, for putting me with the weirdos.

43.
Healer

She walks with Mother Earth,

Her feet firmly grounded.

Her medicine women surround her with their power.

She has a library of wisdom surrounding her,

Ready to be called upon at any time.

Her voice as sweet as an Angel's

And as soothing as being rocked by Mama.

Her eyes an icy blue,

All seeing,

All knowing,

All loving.

She has lips pink like a rose,

Speaking words from a different world.

Her hair –

Its length a reflection of the time she devoted to her magic.

The image of a priestess in all her glory.

44.
INVISIBLE SWORD

I see it in your face.
The decline of your mental health.
Your eyes appear confused,
They can feel the pain but not see the cause.

I can see the invisible knife you hold.
How you turn it in on yourself.
Stabbing right between the breasts,
Deep into the heart.

No blood is spilt from the wound,
No tears are shed.

Not yet.

Soon tears will flow and you won't know why.
Because, my darling friend,
You cannot see the invisible wounds.
You just feel the phantom pain.

It hurts so deep,
You fall to your knees.
Clutching at your chest,
Taking deep breaths.
Begging for it to stop,
The galloping horse in your chest.

Please, my darling friend,
Put down the invisible sword.
Swap it for a shield,
Protect yourself from yourself.
Make friends with the enemy within.

Come home to love again.

'Joy is what happens when we allow ourselves to recognise how good things really are.'

Marianne Williamson

45.
Timeline

We have gone up a level.
Up a level on this whole journey.
How exciting, Love,
How exciting to be on the next stage of this life spiral.

Tell me, Love, what's this next level about?
Well, it's no longer a spiral, it's now a line.
No more visiting old places, we are done.
We just move forward –
As we do, the timeline behind us is washed away.

Sounds a bit like nothingness, Love.
That's exactly what it is –
Nothingness.

Suppose I better get ready for work, Love.
Yes, and take your nothingness with you,
It will get you through the day.

46.
Promotion

I made a deal with Love –
We signed a contract.
We now work together on a permanent basis.
I'm no longer a temporary worker,
It's a permanent role.
It's a good job with amazing benefits.
No pension or annual leave –
Not those kinds.

You see, I was gifted the most precious gift.
She lives there forever and we will also be connected.
A tiny baby, deep within my heart,
She needs nurturing and soothing and playtime too.
She will wake me in the night and leave me tired.
I will always love though it's unconditional.
I will call upon my guide Vemoja if I am unsure of my task.
I feel so lucky, like a lottery winner,
Finally landing my dream job.
Thank you boss aka Love.

47.

Sunshine Sister

There she is –

In the sky shining bright,

My sunshine sister.

Walking above me all day long,

She is always there.

Some days I feel her warmth so much it tingles my skin.

The days I don't feel her I miss her so much.

I try to compensate with the winter jumper and lighting the fire.

The fire is warm but not the same,

It just warms the bit in front,

Not all around me.

The jumper keeps me warm all around but it hangs loose

And gets itchy after a while.

I always knew she would go,

It happens every time.

It's nothing personal,

Just the seasons allowing death and growth.

I cry, "Come back my sunshine sister, I miss your warmth!"

But she doesn't hear me.

She is busy hiding her warmth from the world

Till the time is right.

48.
Full Moon

Full moon stuff.

My heart tells me to go to the beach.

I have a constant image in my soul –

It's the dark sea and full moon reflecting on it.

I make a deal with my heart to go to the beach tonight.

We feel aligned and happy.

Something to look forward to in this lonely home life.

I can feel the energy of the journey start to build and manifest.

The excitement swirling around.

I think about wearing a big cosy jumper and maybe a hat.

I might even take a flask and a blanket.

Oh, this is going to be so romantic and spiritual,

Moon gazing for one.

I then reply to a social media post about full moons.

"I am going to go to the beach," I say.

"Hope you're not going alone," the reply.

"Yes I am," I say with shame.

Shame of having no partner or tribe to go with.

"Well, be careful!" she says.

Now I'm scared and the excitement has shifted
From happy to stupid.

49.
Full Moon Beach Party

The urge to go to the beach was so strong.
The moon and the water calling me
Like a cream cake in the fridge.
I tried to shake it all day long.
But it would not let me be.

I prepared everything I needed and set my intentions.
Picked petals from a rose and used each one as a wish of love
For everyone I know.
I selected some flowers –
White and purple
To be left for the ocean.
It would be magical and spiritual.

The sea was not in sight,
The moon hiding somewhere not to be seen.
I picked my spot and sat down,
Carefully placing the flowers around a candle.
Releasing the petals from my jar.

All the time listening to music,

Not the singing of the mermaids or the angels.

Soul music being played on a stereo by the only other person on the beach.

Who was this man not far from me,

Playing his music,

Dancing,

Being free?

As the sky grew darker I felt a little scared

But also guided by the lights on his stereo.

I then realised I wasn't here for the sea or the moon –

They didn't show up.

I had to speak to the music man.

I picked a beautiful white flower and gathered my things.

I approached him slowly as I didn't want to startle him.

The candle in my Jar lighting me up a little.

He looked at me,

His face wet from crying.

What was his story? I wondered.

He looked me straight in the eyes,

Searching for my soul.

"Thank you for your music," I said and handed him the flower.

95

His face changed from sadness and pain to love and relief.

"Thank you for being here," I said.

Years of worry just lifted from his face.

I can't explain what went on as it was beyond my words.

It felt like his path in life had just taking a new direction.

I smiled and walked away.

And there, in all its glory, the biggest full moon ever.

It was always with me,

Waiting for the right time to show itself.

50.
Here and Now

We are not messing no more.

No more hiding it away.

It's switched on and ready to shine.

What a magical week it turned out to be.

From nothing came everything.

From darkness came light.

From doubt came certainty.

The jigsaw pieces finally connecting together.

When the teacher is ready the students will show.

I am both showing and being shown.

What a wonderful twist in the tale of life.

From blind to all seeing.

From unsure to all knowing.

From deaf to full volume.

Thank you, Love, from my heart to yours.

51.
Circus Girls

Am so glad I didn't know you back then … or am I?
What if we did know each other way back then –
Where would we be now?
We would have run off with the circus,
Travelled the world.

We wouldn't' be performers though,
We would be the added extras.
The one hundred percent living in the moment girls.

I can see us now with our big feather headpiece,
Selling tickets for the show.
Me with a little monkey on my shoulder,
You with a parrot on yours.
Then later on at interval time selling ice cream.
Egging each other on,
Roll up roll up, come and get your ice cream, love.
Big lovely ice cream, love, come and get it.
Having the time of our lives.
Being the world's best sellers.
Easy when everyone remembers us from the ticket sales

And we remember them.

Grabbing those flashes of connections with the people at the show.

The two circus girls living the perfect life in the big top tent.

52.
Inner heaven

I created a healing session.
It came completely from guidance,
Pure divine guidance.
It is designed for people who are locked out of heaven,
Just like I was.
Their own internal heaven shut down,
A reflection of their worldly experiences.

The healing journey starts with setting the intention,
Hand on heart,
Big breaths in.
We start by knocking on heaven's door –
knock knock knocking.
We call in the guides
The medicine women
The Angels
The love
We want in here.to travel with us.
To hold the space and hold our hands.

We go on a journey of commitment,

A ceremony of acceptance.

We walk through the darkness but this time not alone –

We add some forgiveness.

We sit in the fear and watch it pass,

Transmit it into love

And the liquid light fills our hearts.

Committing to our own inner heaven.

Opening the door to our inner love.

Placing the golden healing light in our hearts

To be with us forever.

The process is easy, calm and loving.

The energy continues to be felt every day,

left hand over right on the heart space.

There it is, deep inside.

Strengthened each day through using affirmations and music,

The perfect mix of love.

Affirmations that reflect our closing of the journey

And our own inner heaven.

Not even done it yet but already I'm a MASTER.

53.
Reiki Café

And there it is again, a vision.

Or is it a glimpse into a parallel universe?

The sweetest little cafe painted pale blue and white.

The reiki café by the sea.

A place to top up and be fed.

Little pockets of writers corners to sit and dream the day away.

Beautiful stationary offered as a side to the latte.

Enticing you to write, to connect to that thing called love.

The smiles of the owners filled with gratitude and joy.

Grateful that you trust them with their hearts.

Coming in hungry with an empty feeling.

Going away full, almost overflowing from the feast.

The reiki café, such a special place.

Famous in the What Love Told Me groups all over the world.

A landmark to visit and to sit in awe at all the wonderful books filling the shelves.

Each book a creation from the special writing group.

Not the poets society but the society of love.

In honour of our beautiful friend, sister, angel and mother.
The one who taught us all to be love, have love, feel love and
most importantly show love.

Thank you, Kate.
You are loved,
Accepted,
Appreciated.

'Oh, cock off.'

Katey Roberts

54.
Jesus

I keep thinking about him.

All the time he is popping into my head.

I have never met him,

Well, not physically.

Dear Jesus –

What is it you want me to know?

What are you trying to tell me?

I feel confused with this guy called Jesus.

Why are you stalking my mind?

Are we doing that *Footprints in the Sand* poem?

I can only see one set of footprints –

Were you carrying me?

Is that it?

Do I need carrying right now?

I'm not sure I do, everything feels OKish.

I'm sure all will become clear once I visit my meditation mat

And we have a chat.

With tears burning down my face you can tell me what it is

You want me to know.

55.
Shadows

I feel sad you took what you think is the pain free choice.

Choosing yet again from fear not love.

Unable to heal your sadness as you won't look at it.

I want to scream in your princess face *"fucking wake up and rescue yourself!"*

Numbing your pain with alcohol and nights out.

Returning home to that cold dark bedroom.

The room that reflects your soul, your heart.

You can't face it, that reminder from the room

Of your inner world.

You didn't get a one-night stand yet again as you have tipped over the edge from seductive to scary.

You reach out to friends,

The middle of the night, it doesn't bother you.

I can't stop crying.

When will it all end?

Instead of just saying please rescue me from my self-inflicted sadness by putting my needs above yours.

The same friends' respond, trying to reassure.

Then they reach out to each other as they now have a fear
For your own safety.

The same friends who spent the evening sat alone,
Kids in bed,
Pressing tick and love hearts on your social media photos of the
#nightout
#girlhavingfun.
You see what you did –
You took them on the journey with you.
They were happy with you and now sit in fear with you
But alone.

They are now filled with guilt and worry that they couldn't
come and save you.
They can't sleep because you're not replying.
They don't know that you have fallen asleep,
Now you have had your fill of "I care for you."
Mission complete.
They don't need to save you though,
They need to save themselves from the drunken you.
They are left with a hangover in the morning,
Lack of sleep and worry whilst they press like and love hearts
On your #suchfun #hangover photos.

56.
Flashpoints

I have flashpoints in my life.

It's never just smooth and a gradual getting there.

I always need shifting by the universe.

It's always a big *BOOM* complete change of direction.

It always comes from me,

From a voice within.

I never plan the announcement,

It is always a bombshell.

Like a confession needing to come out but this time my truth.

It's always something that's hidden deep within

And no one has a clue.

Not even me.

It's not always disaster –

Sometimes it's wonderful.

Healing

Energy

Creativity

Knowledge

Love.

It comes from a chemical reaction inside.
Just the right mix of neurons growing new pathways
And firing up.
My life a bit like a science experiment.
It's not such a boom after all –
The formula is being followed.

Add a bit of hurt and a dash of self-love.
Cook for a couple of weeks on the meditation mat.
Throw in some crystals and divine intervention.
Let it rise slowly and see what you become.

57.
Stop Falling

I can feel everyone hurting and it's bring me down.

Made to look like I don't take it serious,

This thing called being sad.

They are all spreading their sadness like gossips spread venom.

I can't be arsed to try and lift you up.

Fall down,

Way down,

Right down to your knees.

Then put the effort in to get back up.

Stop reaching out for the helping hand like a little child.

The child who falls and is lovingly picked back up

Only to run too fast and trip again.

Time for you to walk, not run,

Take in the scenery.

Take notice when your legs begin to wobble

And balance them out.

Stop the inevitable –

Be more present to the other stuff,

Not just the fall.

58.
Sit With Me

If only I was good enough.

If only I could just be me.

No judgement,

No taking things personal.

Really believing my word,

My eyes.

Just let me be happy.

I don't get sad by the darkness.

It's OK that you do.

Please let it be OK that I don't.

I like to sit in it and see what becomes.

I don't see it as punishment,

Or as pain.

No gain without pain, they say.

No dark without light, I reply.

Why choose fear over joy?

It's not a choice, you say.

You already made your choice with that statement.

I am not you,

I am not a pre-programmed being,

Unable to choose my emotions

Just a bundle of pre-set reactions.

Yes, sometimes I forget and then I remember again.

I get it, I truly do,

I have been there.

I have had the pills in my hand and then in my stomach.

Followed by a stomach pump and a belly full of charcoal.

MORE THAN ONCE.

I refuse to let the darkness of the world seep into my skin.

So, for now, I respect your sadness.

I will sit with you for a little bit

But not forever.

Come try and sit with me for a change.

Nobody said it would last forever.

Stop believing it will.

59.
Upside Down.

I am in such a strange place.

I feel upside down.

A thought crossed my mind the other day

That my life is back-to-front.

The awake time is really a dream.

The dream time –

I don't know where that is,

I never remember my dreams.

Maybe the dreams don't happen?

Either way, I am happy –

None of them contain any nightmares.

I feel good and I am happy with my lot.

It's the famous pre-suicide feeling before the deed.

A feeling of all is well and nothing really matters,

No attachment,

Life is meaningless,

No judgements,

No issues.

It's nice, I like it.

Am I detached from reality or connected to love?

'The most terrifying thing is to accept oneself completely.'

Carl Jung

About the Author

You will find Catherine in one of two places – either at work as a nurse, or at home doing healing, writing, cooking, playing the drums, talking to her dog, and being the best mum she can be to her teenage son.

She lives in Lancashire and has one of those Lancashire accents that people recognise instantly. As a reiki master, she is a believer in healing, intention setting, the Law of attraction, igniting the magic within, and choosing love over fear.

Catherine's intention for this book is that it will be placed in the hands of those who need to hear that they can choose again.

Acknowledgements

I want to acknowledge every author, for bravely putting their book out into the world.

To my work colleagues and every healthcare professional in the world for dealing with this pandemic that 2020 brought us.

My wonderful tribe even though, at the moment, we no longer gather together to do our yoga or brunches – I still love and value you all.

Printed in Great Britain
by Amazon